LEOPARD GECKO

The Complete Guide To Setting Up And Maintaining A Healthy Leopard Gecko Tank: A Step-By-Step Guide To Creating The Perfect Environment For Your Pet Reptile

Remy Harrington

Table of Contents

CHAPTER ONE 3
   INTRODUCTION 3
   WHY A PROPER TANK SETUP IS IMPORTANT 6

CHAPTER TWO 10
   CHOOSING THE TANK 10
   GLASS VERSUS PLASTIC TANKS 13
   FRONT-OPENING VERSUS TOP-OPENING TANKS 16

CHAPTER THREE 19
   SUBSTRATE CHOICES 19
   HEATING AND LIGHTING 21
   TEMPERATURE AND MOISTNESS 24

CHAPTER FOUR 30
   HIDING SPOTS AND DECOR 30
   FEEDING AND WATER 33

CHAPTER FIVE 37
   CLEANING AND MAINTENANCE 37
   HANDLING AND ENRICHMENT 40

CHAPTER SIX 45
   WELLBEING AND COMMON ISSUES 45
   SIGNS OF A HEALTHY LEOPARD GECKO 48

CHAPTER SEVEN 53
   BREEDING CONSIDERATIONS 53

THE END 57

CHAPTER ONE

INTRODUCTION

Leopard geckos are perhaps one of the most famous pet reptiles on the planet. They are generally simple to really focus on and make extraordinary pets for both experienced and beginner reptile proprietors. A leopard gecko's tank is a significant piece of their consideration and ought to be set up appropriately to guarantee the wellbeing and prosperity of your pet.

While setting up a leopard gecko's tank, the principal thing to consider is the size. Leopard geckos are little reptiles, so they needn't bother with an enormous tank. A 10-gallon tank is normally adequate for a couple of geckos. The tank ought to likewise have a safe top to keep your gecko from getting away.

The subsequent stage is to pick the substrate. The substrate is the material that lines the lower part of the tank and gives a spot for your gecko to tunnel and stow away. The best substrate for leopard geckos is a blend of sand and soil. This substrate ought to be somewhere around two inches deep to give your gecko adequate room to dig and hide.

When the substrate is set up, you can add a few improvements to the tank. Leopard geckos like to stow away, so adding a few rocks, logs, and other concealing spots is an incredible method for encouraging your gecko. You can likewise add a few live plants to the tank to give it a more regular habitat.

At long last, you'll have to give an intensity source to your gecko. Leopard geckos are cutthroat, so they need a warm climate to remain sound. An intensity light or warming cushion can be utilized to provide essential warmth. The temperature ought to be kept somewhere in the range of 75 and 85 degrees Fahrenheit.

When the tank is set up, you can add your leopard gecko. Try to give a lot of food and water, and screen your gecko's wellbeing consistently. With legitimate consideration, your leopard gecko ought to carry on with a long and solid life.

WHY A PROPER TANK SETUP IS IMPORTANT

A legitimate tank arrangement is critical for leopard geckos since it directly influences their wellbeing and prosperity. These little reptiles might appear to be low-upkeep, yet their habitat plays a critical role in their general personal satisfaction.

Temperature guideline, first and foremost, is vital. Leopard geckos are cutthroat, and that implies they depend on their current circumstances to keep up with their internal heat level. Lack of warming or cooling can prompt pressure, torpidity, and even illness. A legitimate tank arrangement incorporates an intensity source, for example, an under-tank warming cushion or intensity light, alongside a temperature inclination that permits the gecko to move among hotter and cooler regions on a case-by-case basis.

Mugginess control is similarly essential. Leopard geckos come from parched areas and require low mugginess levels to flourish. Extreme dampness can prompt skin and respiratory issues. Keeping up with the right muggy level through legitimate substrate decisions and standard clouding is fundamental to giving a muggy hide.

Substrate determination is another basic angle. Free substrates like sand or rock can prompt impaction, a possibly perilous condition where the gecko ingests substrate while hunting or eating. Selecting safe choices like paper towels, reptile rugs, or record tiles is an unquestionable requirement to forestall this gamble.

Leopard geckos additionally need concealing spots to have a real sense of reassurance. Without legitimate concealing spots, they can end up being focused on and may not eat or act typically. Giving them somewhere around two concealing spots, one on the warm side and one on the cool side, is fundamental to their psychological prosperity.

Moreover, a fittingly estimated tank is essential. Leopard geckos are lone animals; however, they actually need space to move and investigate. A 20-gallon tank is the suggested least size for one grown-up gecko.

CHAPTER TWO
CHOOSING THE TANK

1. Size: Leopard geckos need space to move around. A 20-gallon tank is a decent beginning stage for one gecko; however, in the event that you intend to keep multiple, you'll require a bigger nook. Giving them adequate space is crucial for their prosperity.

2. Material: Tanks made of glass or plastic are appropriate for leopard geckos. Guarantee that the tank has a solid top to forestall getting away and safeguard your gecko from different pets.

3. Ventilation: A legitimate wind current is fundamental to maintaining a sound climate. Pick a nook with

satisfactory ventilation to forestall the development of mugginess and smells.

4. Substrate: Utilize a reasonable substrate for the tank's base. Choices like reptile covers, paper towels, or eco-earth coconut fiber function admirably. Keep away from sand or little particles that can be ingested, causing impaction.

5. Heating and Lighting: Leopard geckos are merciless animals and need an intensity source. Put resources into an under-tank warming cushion or a clay heat producer. They likewise require a day-night cycle; however, abstain from utilizing UVB lighting as they are fundamentally nighttime.

6. Hides: Give no less than two hides—one on the warm side and one on the cooler side of the tank. These concealers offer security for your gecko. You can use commercial reptile hides or make regular-looking safe houses with stopper bark or stones.

7. Temperature Gradient: Keep a temperature inclination inside the tank. The warm side ought to be around 90°F (32°C), while the cooler side ought to be in the low 80s°F (26–28°C). Use a thermostat inside to regulate the temperature.

8. Humidity: Leopard geckos incline toward a dry climate. Keep the moisture level between 20 and 40%. To gauge the

degree of moisture, use a device known as a hygrometer.

9. Decor and Improvement: Add some style, like rocks, branches, and counterfeit plants, to establish a more regular habitat. These likewise give amazing chances to climbing and investigation.

10. Cleaning: Routinely spotless and clean the tank to forestall the development of destructive microorganisms. Eliminate squander and uneaten food and supplant the substrate on a case-by-case basis.

GLASS VERSUS PLASTIC TANKS

Glass tanks are a famous decision for leopard geckos because of their visibility and tasteful allure. They give a reasonable perspective on your pet and can improve the general look of your nook. Nonetheless, there are a few disadvantages to utilizing glass tanks. They can be heavier and more delicate than plastic tanks, making them more challenging to move and possibly simpler to break. Glass tanks can likewise be less productive at keeping up with temperature and stickiness levels, which are pivotal for the prosperity of leopard geckos. They might require extra protection and warming components to establish the best climate.

Then again, plastic tanks, frequently produced using materials like PVC or

ABS, have become progressively well known for lodging leopard geckos. They are lightweight and strong, making them simple to clean and keep up with. Plastic tanks are likewise great at holding intensity and moisture, establishing a more steady and agreeable climate for your gecko. Also, they are less inclined to break if coincidentally dropped or knocked.

At last, the decision between glass and plastic tanks for leopard geckos depends on your needs and spending plan. Glass tanks offer better visibility but may require more work to keep up with temperature and dampness. Plastic tanks are more down to earth with regards to sturdiness and protection.

Whichever you pick, it's fundamental to provide a reasonable substrate, concealing spots, and legitimate lighting to guarantee your leopard gecko's wellbeing and prosperity. Customary cleaning and support are pivotal, no matter what the tank material, to keep your pet blissful and sound.

FRONT-OPENING VERSUS TOP-OPENING TANKS

Front-opening tanks, as the name suggests, have an entryway or access board on the facade of the nook. These tanks give simple access to your leopard gecko and make it advantageous for cleaning, feeding, and handling. The front-opening plan permits you to collaborate with your pet without upsetting its concealing spots, decreasing pressure. Moreover, it's simpler to establish a safe break-resistant climate in a front-opening tank because of the more tight-fitting entryways.

Then again, top-opening tanks highlight a top or top board that you can eliminate to get to the nook. While they can function admirably for leopard geckos, they have a few disadvantages. Top-opening tanks might expect you to disturb your gecko's concealing spots while getting to them, possibly causing pressure. They can likewise be more difficult to get successfully, as leopard geckos are known to be talented climbers and slick people.

Picking either front-opening or top-opening tanks depends on your inclinations and your leopard gecko's necessities. In the event that you value simple entry and decreased pressure for your pet, a front-opening tank is a decent decision. In any case, assuming you as of now have a top-opening tank or find one that suits your necessities, you can make it work by guaranteeing legitimate safety efforts to forestall getaway.

CHAPTER THREE
SUBSTRATE CHOICES

1. Reptile Floor Covering: Reptile cover is a well-known decision for leopard geckos. It's not difficult to spotless, reusable, and gives them a delicate surface to stroll on. Notwithstanding, it tends to be trying to get totally spotless, and microscopic organisms can develop after some time.

2. Paper Towels/Newspaper: These are the most reasonable and simple-to-clean choices. Essentially, supplant them when ruined. Nonetheless, they don't offer a lot of footing for your gecko, and they may not look as stylishly satisfying.

3. Tile: Smooth tiles are another fantastic choice. They're not difficult to spot, are solid, and assist with managing your gecko's nails normally. Ensure the tiles aren't excessively dangerous, and keep away from harsh-finished tiles that can hurt their skin.

4. Slate or Flagstone: These level stones give a characteristic appearance as well as assist with keeping up with legitimate temperatures. Guarantee they're safely positioned to keep your gecko from tunneling under.

5. Cohesive Sand: Try not to utilize free sand, as it tends to be ingested by your gecko, prompting impaction. Strong sand, for example, play sand, can be utilized yet ought to be blended in

with different substrates to lessen ingestion risk.

6. Reptile-Explicit Substrates: Monetarily accessible substrates like calcium sand and eco-earth are intended for reptiles. While they can be reasonable, consistently screen your gecko for any ingestion issues.

7. Mixed Substrates: A few guardians select a blend of substrates like eco-earth and record to give both surface and dampness control.

HEATING AND LIGHTING
Heating:

1. Under Tank Heater (UTH): The essential intensity hotspot for leopard geckos is an under-tank warmer. Put it

on one side of the enclosure, covering roughly 33% of the tank's floor. This makes a temperature slope, permitting your gecko to pick its favored temperature.

2. Thermostat Control: Consistently utilize an indoor regulator with the UTH to keep a reliable and safe temperature. Set the temperature to around 88–92°F (31-33°C) on the warm side and 75–80°F (24–27°C) on the cooler side.

3. Heat Mat Arrangement: Guarantee that the intensity mat is put outside the enclosure, under the tank. This prevents direct contact between the gecko and the warming component.

Lighting:

1. Day-Night Cycle: Leopard geckos don't need UVB lighting like a few different reptiles. They are crepuscular, meaning they are generally dynamic during sunrise and sunset. A normal day-night pattern of 12 hours of light and 12 hours of dimness is adequate.

2. Low-Level Lighting: Utilize a low-wattage, non-UVB bulb for lighting during the day. This gives a delicate light source without upsetting your gecko's regular way of behaving.

3. Nighttime Dimness: Mood killer all lighting during the night to give a time of haziness to your gecko. This mirrors their regular habitat and manages their circadian rhythms.

Extra Tips:

1. Temperature Observing: Consistently check the temperatures in your gecko's nook using a dependable thermometer. This guarantees the intensity source is working accurately.

2. Heat Hide: Spot a hide or cover over the warm side of the nook. This gives your gecko a safe and warm spot to withdraw to when required.

3. Avoid Direct Daylight: Get the enclosure far from direct daylight, as it can prompt overheating and distress for your gecko.

TEMPERATURE AND MOISTNESS
Temperature:

1. Basking Spot: Furnish a relaxing spot with a temperature range of 88–92°F (31-33°C). This region permits your gecko to heat up and helps with absorption.

2. Cool Side: The furthest edge of the tank ought to have a cooler temperature, preferably around 70–80°F (21-27°C). This gives your gecko a decision to thermoregulate.

3. Nighttime Drop: Leopard geckos need an evening tempcrature decrease. This can be in the range of 70–75°F (21–24°C).

4. Heat Source: You can accomplish these temperature ranges by utilizing under-tank warming cushions or artistic

intensity producers. Keep away from hot rocks, as they can cause consumption.

Moistness:

1. Desert Circumstances: Leopard geckos come from parched districts, so they require low stickiness levels. Hold back the moisture in the tank.

2. Shedding Guide: Marginally expanded moistness (40–60%) during shedding can assist them with shedding their skin all the more without any problem. Give a muggy cover to the saturated sphagnum greenery.

Monitoring:

1. Thermometers and Hygrometers: Utilize solid, advanced thermometers

and hygrometers to monitor temperature and dampness levels. Place them at various spots in the tank to guarantee exactness.

2. Regular Checks: Practice it all the time to actually look at these readings every day to guarantee they stay inside the suggested ranges.

Tips:

1. Gradient Setup: Make a temperature gradient in the tank, with the luxuriating spot being the hottest and the cool side being cooler. This permits your gecko to pick its preferred temperature.

2. Substrate: Pick a substrate like reptile floor covering or paper towels

that don't hold dampness, as overabundance of moistness can prompt respiratory issues.

3. Water Dish: Consistently give a spotless water dish, yet guarantee it doesn't add to overabundance stickiness. Place it on the tank's cooler side.

Keeping up with the right temperature and stickiness levels in your leopard gecko's tank is fundamental for their general wellbeing and solace. Giving a legitimate temperature slope and observing these levels reliably will assist with guaranteeing your pet flourishes in its nook. Continuously research and talk with a reptile veterinarian to meet the particular requirements of your leopard gecko, as individual geckos might have somewhat various inclinations.

CHAPTER FOUR
HIDING SPOTS AND DECOR

1. Hide Boxes: Leopard geckos are nighttime animals that need concealing spots during the day. Utilize small, secure concealment boxes made of materials like plastic or wood. Place one on the warm side and one more on the cooler side of the tank to accommodate their temperature inclinations.

2. Substrate: Pick a reasonable substrate like a reptile cover, paper towels, or tile for the tank's floor. Keep away from free substrates like sand, as ingestion can prompt medical problems.

3. Heat Source: Introduce an under-tank warming cushion or intensity light with an indoor regulator to keep up with

the tank's temperature. Position it on one side of the nook to make a warm slope.

4. Decorative Components: Leopard geckos value some visual excitement. Add protected and simple-to-clean styles like rocks, counterfeit plants, and branches. These things additionally give climbing valuable open doors and copy their regular habitat.

5. Lighting: Leopard geckos don't need UVB lighting but will profit from a normal day-night cycle. Utilize a low-wattage bulb for light during the day and turn it off around evening time.

6. Water Bowl: Give a shallow and effectively open water bowl. Keep it clean and give it new water routinely.

7. Feeding Region: Spot an assigned feeding dish or stage to keep bugs and worms contained while your gecko eats. This makes cleanup simpler.

8. Cleaning Daily practice: Consistently clean the tank to maintain a sterile climate. Eliminate squander, supplant ruined substrate, and sanitize stylistic layout things when important.

9. Minimalistic Methodology: Try not to stuff the fenced-in area with enrichments. Leopard geckos need more than adequate floor space for development.

10. Observation: Invest energy in noticing your gecko's way of behaving and changing the tank arrangement appropriately. Assuming they appear to be focused on or awkward, consider tweaking their concealing spots or adornments.

FEEDING AND WATER

Feeding:

Leopard geckos are insectivores, and that implies their essential diet consists of bugs. The fundamental food things for your gecko incorporate crickets, mealworms, waxworms, and bugs. Ensure the bugs you offer are properly estimated, no bigger than the width of your gecko's head, to forestall stifling.

Feed your leopard gecko each and every other day when they're adults and each day when they're adolescents. Offer them however many bugs they can consume in around 15–20 minutes. It's important not to overload and to stay away from heaviness.

Make sure to tidy up the bugs with a calcium supplement, something like once per week, and a multivitamin supplement each and every week to guarantee your gecko gets the fundamental supplements. Place these enhancements in a little dish in their nook for them to lick, depending on the situation.

Water:

Leopard geckos get a large portion of their hydration from the bugs they eat. Nonetheless, it's significant to have a shallow water dish in their nook to guarantee they approach clean water consistently. The dish ought to be sufficiently shallow to forestall suffocating, however huge enough for your gecko to serenely drink.

Change the water in the dish from day to day to keep it perfect and liberated from flotsam and jetsam. Utilize dechlorinated water, as faucet water with chlorine or different synthetic compounds can be destructive to your gecko's wellbeing.

Clouding the nook with water periodically can likewise assist with keeping up with stickiness levels and give extra hydration to your gecko. In any case, ensure the nook doesn't turn out to be excessively clammy, as leopard geckos usually like a somewhat dry climate.

CHAPTER FIVE

CLEANING AND MAINTENANCE

1. Frequency of Cleaning: Leopard gecko tanks ought to be cleaned on a customary timetable. A careful cleaning ought to be done twice a month, while spot cleaning should be possible from day to day to eliminate squander.

2. Remove the Gecko: Prior to beginning the cleaning system, cautiously eliminate your leopard gecko from its nook and spot it in a solid transitory holder with proper temperature and concealing spots.

3. Empty the Tank: Take out every one of the extras, for example, hides, water dishes, and beautifications.

Discard any uneaten food and excrement.

4. Clean the Substrate: In the event that you utilize a free substrate like coconut coir or calcium sand, scoop out the filthy regions and supplant them with new substrate. Assuming you use paper towels or reptile rugs, eliminate and replace them.

5. Wash Embellishments and Frill: Clean and sanitize all tank beautifications, including stows and branches, with warm water and a gentle reptile-safe sanitizer. Wash completely to eliminate any buildup.

6. Clean the Tank Walls: Wipe down the walls of the tank with a reptile-safe

glass cleaner or a combination of water and white vinegar to eliminate any smirches or development.

7. Sanitize the Water Dish: Wash the water dish with hot, sudsy water, flush completely, and top off with new dechlorinated water.

8. Check Heating and Lighting: Assess warming components and lighting installations for any harm or glitch. Supplant any defective hardware.

9. Return Embellishments: Spot the cleaned and dried enhancements, stow away, and water dish once again into the tank. Guarantee that there are suitable concealing spots and a relaxing region.

10. Temperature and Moistness: Restore appropriate temperature and moisture levels in the tank. Utilize a computerized thermometer and hygrometer to screen for these circumstances.

11. Add Your Gecko: Tenderly spot your leopard gecko back into its perfect and agreeable walled-in area.

12. Regular: In the middle of profound cleanings, perform everyday spot checks for squander expulsion and guarantee the water dish is perfect and full.

HANDLING AND ENRICHMENT

1. Tank Arrangement: Begin with a 20-gallon tank for a solitary leopard gecko, and add 10 gallons for each extra

gecko. Guarantee the tank has a safe top to forestall getting away.

2. Substrate: Utilize a substrate like a reptile cover, paper towels, or non-glue rack liner for the tank base. This makes cleaning more straightforward and keeps impaction from ingested free substrates.

3. Heating and Lighting: Keep a temperature slope in the tank. Utilize an under-tank warming cushion on one side to make a warm spot around 90°F (32°C) and keep the opposite side cooler at around 75-80°F (24-27°C). Give a low-wattage heat lamp for relaxing. Utilize an UVB light to support calcium digestion yet guarantee it's not areas of

excessive strength; leopard geckos are for the most part crepuscular.

4. Hideouts: Spot different concealing spots, similar to half logs or business stows, in the tank. These provide your gecko with the conviction that all is well.

5. Water and Hydration: Give a shallow dish of fresh, clean water. Leopard geckos chiefly get their hydration from their food, so a water dish is basically for drenching.

6. Feeding: Feed your gecko a diet of stomach-stacked bugs like crickets, mealworms, or dubia insects. Dust the bugs with a calcium supplement routinely. Feed adolescents day to day and adults each and every other day.

7. Enrichment: Change up their diet by periodically offering waxworms, silkworms, or different bugs. You can likewise present various kinds of stows, branches, or shakes to establish a seriously intriguing climate.

8. Handling: Leopard geckos are by and large mild, yet handle them delicately and rarely to diminish pressure. Clean up prior to handling, and stay away from unexpected developments. Handle them for brief periods and regard their craving to withdraw to their hide.

9. Cleaning: Spot-clean the tank day to day by eliminating waste. Plays out a full tank clean every 2 to 4 weeks, contingent upon the substrate utilized.

Sanitize and wash all things completely during cleaning.

10. Health Checking: Watch out for your gecko's way of behaving, hunger, and shedding. Any radical changes might demonstrate medical problems. Counsel a reptile veterinarian in the event that you suspect any issues.

CHAPTER SIX

WELLBEING AND COMMON ISSUES

1. Temperature and Lighting: Leopard geckos require a warm climate. Guarantee their nook has a temperature inclination, with a lounging spot around 90–95°F (32–35°C) and a cooler region around 75–80°F (24–27°C). Utilize an intensity source like an under-tank warmer and give an UVB light to legitimate calcium ingestion.

2. Housing: Utilize a properly estimated tank with secure covers. Abstain from congestion, as leopard geckos are single creatures. Give concealing spots damp stows away for shedding and dry stows away for rest.

3. Diet: Feed a diet of live bugs, basically crickets, mealworms, and Dubai cockroaches. Dust the prey with calcium and nutrient enhancements. Try not to take care of bugs trapped in the wild, as these may carry parasites.

4. Hydration: Leopard geckos generally get water from their food, yet give them a shallow water dish to guarantee they approach new water consistently.

5. Shedding: Leopard geckos shed their skin occasionally. Guarantee legitimate mugginess levels (around 40-half) and furnish a damp stowaway to assist with shedding. Eliminate any held shed to forestall entanglements.

6. Normal medical problems:

• Impaction: This happens when a gecko ingests substrate or non-edible materials. Use paper towels or reptile covers as substrates to forestall this.

• Respiratory Diseases: Keep the nook clean and keep up with appropriate stickiness levels to forestall respiratory issues. Signs incorporate wheezing and nasal release.

• Metabolic Bone Sickness (MBD): Lack of calcium admission can prompt MBD. Guarantee legitimate supplementation and UVB lighting to forestall this devastating condition.

• Parasites: Consistently check for indications of parasites like weight reduction, dormancy, or unusual dung. Counsel a vet on the off chance that you suspect a pervasive

7. Regular Vet Check-ups: Schedule standard check-ups with a reptile veterinarian to screen your gecko's wellbeing and address any issues quickly.

SIGNS OF A HEALTHY LEOPARD GECKO

1. Active and Alert: A solid leopard gecko is dynamic during its evening hours (they are nighttime) and ought to seem ready when conscious. It will investigate its nook, flicking its tongue to smell and taste its environmental factors.

2. Good Body Condition: Your gecko ought to have a stout, adjusted tail and a proportional body. A perceptible loss of muscle-to-fat ratio or a slight tail could demonstrate medical problems.

3. Clear Eyes: The gecko's eyes ought to be clear and liberated from any release or darkness. Overcast or enlarged eyes can be an indication of disease or injury.

4. Healthy Skin: The skin ought to be smooth and liberated from any apparent injuries, wounds, or scraped areas. Leopard geckos can shed their skin, and it's typical for them to seem dull prior to shedding.

5. Proper Weight: A solid leopard gecko ought to have a moderate and steady weight. Consistently check its weight using a limited scale to guarantee it's not losing or acquiring an excess of weight.

6. Shedding Appropriately: Shedding is a characteristic interaction for leopard geckos. They ought to shed their skin in one piece with next to no challenges. Stuck-out skin can prompt medical problems.

7. Good Appetite: A sound gecko will have a predictable and solid hunger. They are insectivores, so they ought to promptly consume live bugs like crickets, mealworms, or Dubai cockroaches.

8. Proper Temperature and Lighting: Guarantee your gecko's fenced-in area keeps up with the fitting temperature and lighting. Leopard geckos require a relaxing spot with an intensity source and a cooler side for thermoregulation.

9. Hydration: Give a shallow dish of spotless, new water consistently. Despite the fact that leopard geckos don't drink as much as a few different reptiles, they might, in any case, sometimes hydrate.

10. Clean Climate: Routinely spotless and clean the gecko's walled-in area to forestall the development of microscopic organisms and parasites.

11. Stress-Free Behavior: Solid leopard geckos shouldn't show indications of

stress, like over-the-top stowing away, loss of hunger, or a forceful way of behaving.

12. Regular Shedding: Leopard geckos shed their skin routinely, so you ought to see proof of shed skin in their nook.

CHAPTER SEVEN

BREEDING CONSIDERATIONS

1. Age and Wellbeing: Guarantee that both the male and female leopard geckos are experienced and healthy prior to endeavoring to raise them. They ought to be no less than 9 to a year old and have arrived at the very least weight of 45 grams.

2. Housing: Give separate nooks to the male and female geckos. These ought to be sufficiently measured with fitting warming and lighting. Legitimate temperature and dampness are pivotal for fruitful reproduction.

3. Introduction: When you are prepared to raise, acquaint the male with the female's nook, not the opposite

way around. Manage their connections to forestall forceful ways of behaving, which can prompt wounds.

4. Copulation: Mating normally happens around evening time. The male will move toward the female and endeavor to embed his hemipenes. This interaction can be very forceful, so screen them near to guarantee it goes without a hitch.

5. Egg-Laying: After fruitful sexual intercourse, the female will lay eggs, normally within two to about a month. Give her a reasonable egg-laying box loaded with sodden, vermiculite, or perlite substrate for her to lay her eggs in.

6. Incubation: Cautiously gather the eggs and spot them in a hatchery set to a temperature between 80 and 88°F (27 and 31°C) for roughly 45 to 60 days. Screen stickiness levels to forestall drying out or contagious development on the eggs.

7. Hatchlings: When the eggs hatch, be ready to really focus on the hatchlings. They are delicate and will require more modest nooks with fitting warmth and lighting. Feed them fittingly estimated bugs like little crickets or mealworms.

8. Healthcare: Routinely screen the soundness of your reproducing pair and their posterity. Be ready to isolate any

geckos that give indications of an ailment or animosity.

9. Genetics: In the event that you are reproducing for explicit characteristics or transformations, comprehend the hereditary qualities included. Research the hereditary qualities of leopard geckos to foresee the likely results of your reproducing matches.

10. Ethical Contemplations: Consistently consider the prosperity of the creatures regardless of anything else. Keep away from exorbitant rearing and overproduction of geckos, as this can prompt packed covers and undesirable creatures.

THE END

Printed in Great Britain
by Amazon